# ice dancing

Anna Claybourne
with Liz Gogerly

Lerner Publications Company
**Minneapolis**

First American edition published in 2012 by Lerner Publishing Group, Inc. Published by arrangement with Wayland, a division of Hachette Children's Books

Lerner Publications Company
A division of Lerner Publishing Group, Inc.
241 First Avenue North
Minneapolis, MN U.S.A.

Website address: www.lernerbooks.com

Library of Congress Cataloging-in-Publication Data
Claybourne, Anna.
    Ice dancing / by Anna Claybourne.
      p.   cm. — (On the radar–dance)
    Includes index.
    ISBN 978-0-7613-7765-8 (lib. bdg. : alk. paper)
    1. Ice dancers. 2. Ice dancing. I. Title.
GV850.45.C53 2012
796.91'2—dc22                          2011002416

Manufactured in the United States of America
—CG—7/15/11

Photo Acknowledgments
Images in this book are used with the permission of: Alamy: Amoret Tanner 7; Corbis: Jean-Yves Ruszniewski/TempSport; Stewart Feinstein: 20–21, 26–27; Flickr: Dave Wharton Photography 4–5; Philip Rees Photography: 14; Shutterstock: Almotional 31, Diego Barbieri 9, 12cl, 25tr, Galina Barskaya 25bc, Olga Besnard 1, 12bl, 22–23, 24r, 25tl, Songguan Deng 19, Gertan 10, André Klaassen 13tl, Testing cover, 6, 3bl, 13cr, 16br, 16tr, Valeria73 17; Wikipedia: Caroline Paré 3br.

Main body text set in Helvetica Neue LT Std 13/15.5. Typeface provided by Adobe Systems.

# cover stories

# thepeople

# themoves

# thetalk

# DANCING ON THE ICE!

Graceful dance moves, aerial jumps and lifts, and incredibly fast spins make figure skating challenging and impressive to watch. Performing on the ice requires strength and fitness, perfect timing, and highly expressive body movements.

Figure skating disciplines include freestyle, pairs, ice dancing, and synchronized skating. Each has its own special rules, techniques, and skills.

## Freestyle

Energetic and exciting, freestyle skating is full of spectacular jumps and spins. Freestyle is performed by a solo (single) skater.

## Pairs

Male and female skaters perform together in pairs skating. They can skate together or apart, but their movements, including jumps and spins, must be perfectly synchronized, with matching footwork, body shapes, and even facial expressions!

## Ice dancing

Without the dramatic spins and lifts of freestyle and pairs skating, ice dancers perform ballroom-style moves on the ice. Music is very important, with skaters telling a story through their flowing body shapes and constant changes of direction.

## Synchronized skating

This style can involve up to 20 skaters at one time performing perfectly synchronized dance routines on the ice.

# Skating stars on ice!

*Stars on Ice* is an award-winning ice-dancing show that features the talents of Olympic and world championship skaters. Men and women skaters perform solo numbers of their own choosing. They also skate as an elite ensemble to artistically choreographed music and moves. The touring show appears in cities throughout the United States and Canada, as well as in Japan, South Korea, and Mexico.

# THE STORY OF SKATING

The oldest pair of skates dates back to about 5,000 years ago. They were found at the bottom of a lake in Switzerland. Made from the leg bones of large animals, the skates had holes at each end of the bone. Leather straps were used to tie on the skates.

## Skates get an update

In the 1300s, the Dutch started using wooden skates with flat pieces of iron attached to the bottom. They were tied to the shoes with leather straps, and skaters would push themselves across the ice with a long pole. Two hundred years later, a narrow metal blade was added, allowing the skater to push and glide with his feet without using a pole.

## The first skating club

The world's first skating club was formed almost 300 years ago in Edinburgh, Scotland. To join, candidates had to skate simple shapes (or figures) and jump over three hats piled on top of one another!

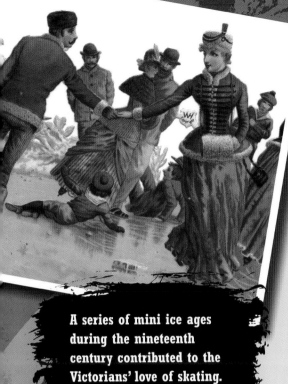

A series of mini ice ages during the nineteenth century contributed to the Victorians' love of skating. People flocked to skate on Britain's frozen lakes.

## Trailblazer

U.S. ballet dancer and skater Jackson Haines is credited with inventing modern figure skating in the 1860s. Wearing the skates he had invented (with blades screwed directly into the soles of his boots), Haines entertained crowds with his athletic jumps and spins. His speciality, the sit spin, is still one of the basic spin types.

## Waltzing on ice

The discipline of ice dancing developed as a sport in the 1930s. The first skaters performed dances such as the tango, the fox-trot, and the waltz on ice.

## U.S., Soviet, and Russian Olympians

Beginning in the mid-1900s, the United States enjoyed strong Olympic success in men's and ladies' singles. U.S. skaters earned 14 gold medals—seven in each singles competition. Meanwhile, Soviet (and later Russian) teams have dominated pairs skating, winning gold in every Olympic Games from 1964 through 2002. They have also had strong success in ice dancing, earning gold in seven of the last 10 Olympic competitions.

## Eastern promise

Ice skating has seen a huge surge in popularity in Asia, particularly in Japan, China, and South Korea. At the 2010 World Figure Skating Championships in Italy, China took the gold in the pairs skating, and Japan took gold in the men's and ladies' singles. At the 2010 Winter Olympics, Mao Asada of Japan became the first woman to land three triple axel jumps in the same competition.

# SPICE UP THE ICE!

Are you looking for a hobby that combines dance, drama, speed, skill, and strength? Try figure skating! Here are some of the reasons why you should get your skates on.

**1**

The best ice dancers come alive in front of an audience, losing themselves in the music and movement and creating a wonderful spectacle. If you enjoy performing and love dressing up in colorful, eye-catching outfits, this is the hobby for you!

**2**

Ice skating is fantastic exercise. One hour performing on the ice is the equivalent of a 5-mile (8-kilometer) run. The sport raises your heart rate, works your stomach muscles, strengthens your thighs, and even exercises your shoulders and upper arms. Skating also improves your balance and increases your stamina too.

**3**

Figure skating is a year-round hobby. During the winter months, outdoor rinks or frozen ponds and lakes are great places to go and have fun with your friends. For the rest of the year, you can head indoors to your local ice rink. The fun never has to stop!

**4** Work hard and keep practicing, and you could turn a fun hobby into an exciting career. Apart from competing in events such as the World Championships and Winter Olympics, professional skaters perform around the world in exhibitions, traveling ice shows, and even on television. Imagine being paid to do something you love!

**5** Performing on the ice is something you can do for a lifetime. Skaters as young as 15 have won Olympic medals, and ice dancing is a great way for older people to stay healthy and to have fun. Even though some of the falls look spectacular, it's a hobby with relatively few injuries.

Ice skating can be anything you want it to be—fast, exciting, physical, graceful, controlled, or glamorous. Skaters can go it alone, pair up with a partner, or even become part of a huge synchronized team. There's something for everyone to enjoy. What are you waiting for? Spice up the ice!

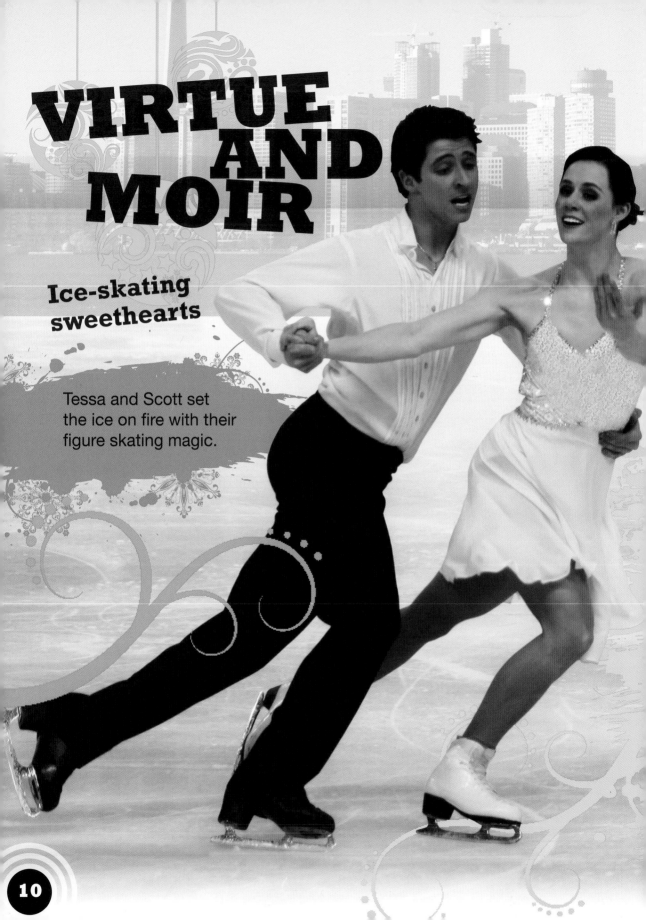

# VIRTUE AND MOIR

## Ice-skating sweethearts

Tessa and Scott set the ice on fire with their figure skating magic.

**THE STATS**
**Name:** Tessa Virtue
**Born:** May 17, 1989
**Place of birth:** London, Ontario, Canada
**Job:** Competitive ice skater

**THE STATS**
**Name:** Scott Moir
**Born:** September 2, 1987
**Place of birth:** London, Ontario, Canada
**Job:** Competitive ice skater

## First meeting

Tessa was just seven and Scott was nine years old when they first began skating together. Scott's family ran an ice-skating camp, and his aunt paired him with Tessa for competitions. Scott was really into ice hockey and ice skating. But when the time came, he chose to concentrate on skating—and started down a path to ice rink superstardom!

## Junior champs

It soon became clear that Scott and Tessa were something special. As teenagers, they competed at the junior level and won 10 gold medals, three silvers, and three bronzes at Canadian and World Championships—including gold at the World Junior Championships in 2006.

## Moving on up

From 2006 Tessa and Scott competed at the senior level. By the end of the 2009–2010 season, they had won 17 medals at international and national level—nine of them gold! They came first in ice dancing in the Canadian Figure Skating Championships three times in a row, becoming celebrities in Canada.

## Olympic gold

Tessa and Scott made their Olympic debut at the 2010 Winter Olympics in Vancouver, Canada. Stunning the home audience with a flawless and breathtakingly beautiful free dance, Canada's ice-skating sweethearts became the first ice dancers to win gold at their very first Olympic Games.

# THE SPINS

layback spin

camel spin

From spectacular uprights to complicated camels, spins are used to add drama and grace to a performance. Here are some of the most popular:

## Layback spin

This graceful upright spin is usually performed by a female skater. The hips are pushed forward, allowing the back to bend. The skater extends her head and neck while supporting her weight on one leg and lifting the free leg behind her. The arms are raised in a balletlike pose.

## Camel spin

In this spin, the body forms a T shape. The free leg is stretched out behind while the skater balances on the spinning leg. The camel spin requires good technique, timing, and balance.

## Biellmann spin

This breathtaking upright move starts with the skater spinning with one leg raised. The skater bends to the side to take hold of the blade with one hand and pulls the leg backward and up. The skater then holds the blade with both hands to pull it up behind the head. This spin requires great flexibility.

## Sit spin

This is a spin performed in a sitting position. The skater's rear should not be higher than the level of the supporting knee. The free leg is usually extended out in front. The upper part of the spinning leg must be parallel to the ice.

## Haircutter spin

This is a variation of the layback spin, but the free skate is brought toward the head. The blade gets close enough to "cut" the skater's hair!

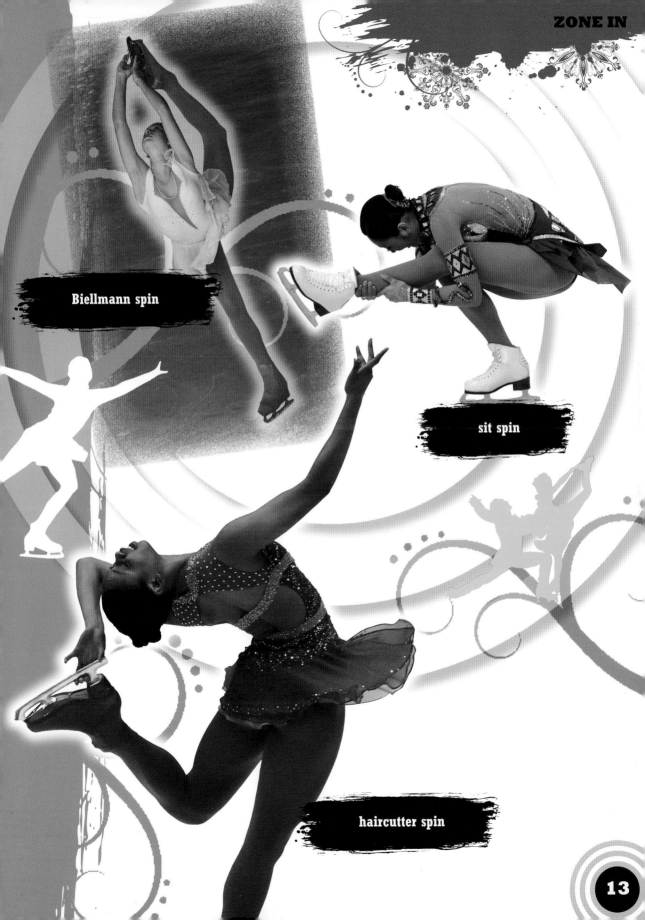

Biellmann spin

sit spin

haircutter spin

# PARTY ON ICE

## My story by Zoe Rees

My very first skating memories are quite embarrassing! My friends were into ice-skating birthday parties, and it seemed like everyone could skate except me. I was so bad my mom had to hold my hand and help me around the rink! I was determined to get better though, and at 10 years old I started lessons.

The first stage was joining a beginners' course at my local rink. The idea was you mastered the basics one level at a time. When you passed, you moved on to the next level. I picked things up quickly and soon felt much more confident on the ice. When I was 11, I won a Most Improved Skater award from my club. I'd only been learning for a year, and so winning was the best feeling ever.

Now I'm at the rink four times a week for up to four hours each time! I'm practicing for skating exams. At the moment I'm mastering double jumps! I really want to be a coach one day. That's something I'm working toward now.

Figure skating has taught me that hard work and determination pay off. If you get something wrong, you just have to pick yourself up and keep on trying. Skating's a brilliant hobby that has helped me to make lots of great friends and keep me really fit. And if anyone invites me to a party on ice these days, I let my mom stay at home!

# ICE SPEAK

Don't head to the rink until you've read On the Radar's ice speak guide!

**blade**
the metal part of a skate that makes contact with the ice

**double axel**
a jump with a forward takeoff. The skater does two and a half spins in the air and lands facing backward.

**double jump**
a jump that involves two rotations in the air before landing

**edges**
the fine ridges of steel on either side of a skate blade

**edge work**
precise footwork on skates, performed on the edges of the blade

**figure skating**
an artistic sport that includes several disciplines. They showcase jumps, dances, lifts, spins, and figures.

**free dance**
an ice dance program in which the dancers choose their music and make up their own routines and moves

**free program**
a competition performance that lasts four minutes and 30 seconds for men and four minutes for women

**freestyle**
a figure skating discipline in which skaters are free to add lifts, spins, and jumps to their programs

**ice dancing**
a figure skating discipline in which a man and a woman perform versions of ballroom dances on ice

**pairs**
when a male skater and a female skater perform together

**quad/ quadruple**
a jump in which the skater spins around four times in the air before landing

**rink**
an indoor or outdoor expanse of ice used for ice skating

**short program**
a competition performance that lasts no longer than two minutes and 50 seconds

### singles
solo skating

### split scissor
an aerial pose where the legs are open like a pair of scissors

### step sequences
quick changes of direction and foot movements used to travel around the ice

### stroking
a term used to describe moving from one skate to the other to travel across the ice

### triple axel
a jump with a forward takeoff. The skater does three and a half spins in the air and lands facing backward

# GLOSSARY

### complex carbohydrates
energy-giving foods such as bread, rice, and pasta

### consecutive
following one after the other

### finale
the end part of a performance

### ice age
a time when parts of Earth became dramatically colder and were covered with snow and ice

### invigorate
to be filled with energy

### momentum
an impelling force or strength of movement

### seasonal
happening only at certain times of the year

### stamina
the ability to do something for a long time

### synchronize
when body movements are coordinated, often in time to music

# THE NEW ICE AGE

Go downtown or to tourist spots around the world, and you are likely to find an ice rink nearby. Where did the idea come from, and what effect is it having on the popularity of skating? Read on to find out.

## Starting the trend

The granddaddy of all outdoor skating venues is the Ice Skating Rink at Rockefeller Center in New York. Built in 1936, it attracts a quarter of a million people every winter! Skaters also flock to the open-air Wollman Rink in the city's famous Central Park.

## Find the magic!

In some parts of the United States and Canada, outdoor skating takes place on lakes, rivers, and canals that have frozen over during the winter. (Be sure to check that skating is safe on these natural rinks.) Some families even install a backyard rink of their own! U.S. Olympic figure skater Peggy Fleming, has said that "Lake Placid, New York, was my first exposure to skating outdoors on natural ice. The feeling of the cool breeze on your face outdoors is magical."

## Crowd-pulling fun!

Seasonal rinks can be expensive to build and maintain. Nevertheless, their numbers keep growing around the world. Rinks have opened in San Francisco's Union Square, at the Boston Common Frog Pond, in Berlin's Potsdamer Platz, and even at the Eiffel Tower in Paris! Local businesses see the rinks as a great way to attract crowds who will also do a bit of shopping when they take off their skates.

## The ice bug

Seasonal ice rinks are here to stay. The result of this improved access to ice rinks is that more people are being bitten by the skating bug. If you pull on a pair of skates for the first time under the moonlight, overlooked by wonderful historical buildings, in major tourist spots, or in a buzzing downtown area, skating becomes magic, fantasy, and fun! And the chances are you'll want to go back again and again.

With the famous cityscape of New York in the background, the Wollman Rink is popular with tourists and New Yorkers alike.

# A WEEK IN THE LIFE OF INTERNATIONAL SKATER

# JONO PARTRIDGE

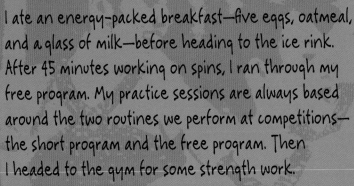

**blog**  **news**  **events**

## Monday

I ate an energy-packed breakfast—five eggs, oatmeal, and a glass of milk—before heading to the ice rink. After 45 minutes working on spins, I ran through my free program. My practice sessions are always based around the two routines we perform at competitions—the short program and the free program. Then I headed to the gym for some strength work.

## Tuesday

My training today focused on jumps, spins, and step sequences. After doing my steps, it was back home for a healthy dinner—fish, brown rice, and steamed vegetables. My diet is based around protein and complex carbohydrates for energy.

## Wednesday

I was on the ice by 9:00 a.m. today to practice my jumps. It's best to get to the rink when the ice has just been resurfaced. Fresh ice is more springy and far blog    news    events

better for jumping. Where I train in Colorado, the ice is resurfaced every 45 minutes.

## Thursday

Tomorrow is competition day! I had four sessions on the ice today of 45 minutes each. I focused on the most difficult parts from each program. I wanted everything to be perfect—like I could do it in my sleep! Then I did three 20-minute stretching sessions to warm down and stay flexible.

## Friday

The big day's finally here! I had a stretching session in the morning and worked through my jumps in my head. They are the hardest things to get right. The triple axel is the hardest jump in the world! My short program went well, and my score was a personal best, so I felt good.

## Saturday

Today was the free program competition. I didn't skate as well as I know I can. My nerves got to me, and I just didn't feel loose. It was frustrating because the moves were coming out perfectly in practice all week! But I still ended the competition with a new personal best score, which was great. On Monday morning, I'll start all over again!

# COMPETITION FEVER!

You take a deep breath and move toward the center of the ice. A hush falls over the crowd, the lights go down, and the judges straighten in their seats. You strike your starting pose, eyes down, feet turned out, arms by your sides. The lights sparkle on your costume like a thousand tiny diamonds. You're as still as a statue, but your heart pounds in your chest like a drum. It's time to begin.

## Glassy rink

You hear the first few notes of the music. It's lively and exhilarating, perfect for the routine you've been practicing for months. The hours you've spent on the ice immediately kick in, and your body responds as if by remote control. The ice is fresh, your blades are sharp, and your body feels strong and supple. It's like you're gliding on glass as you work your way around the rink.

## Ice magic

You feel the cool air hit your face, and it invigorates you, sending a magical feeling flowing through your veins and making your pulse race. Every pore in your body is working toward one goal, the ultimate performance. It's intense, as if you were floating on air. You turn and spin with ease and then glide beautifully like a graceful swan. The audience and judges drift away from your mind as you move toward your finale.

## Skate gold

The next thing you know, you're lifting off, soaring, spinning, once, twice, three times! Time stands still, and there is only you, the air, the ice, and the moment. You land perfectly. Then the noise starts to build. The sound of clapping and cheering fills your ears and brings tears to your eyes. You've done it—a gold medal for a winning performance.

# THE LIFTS & THE JUMPS

Lifts and jumps are an important part of figure skating. Get them right, and you add drama, excitement, and judges' points to your routine. Here are just a few the experts use:

## Throw jump

This is a dramatic pairs move, in which the man throws the woman into the air. She spins and lands on her own.

## Lasso lift

In this lift, the couple begin by holding hands as they skate. The man then lifts the woman around his back and above his head (as though he is swinging a lasso!).

## Twist lift

This pairs move starts with the couple skating backward. The man holds the woman around the waist, lifts her off the ice, and throws her into the air. The woman spins horizontally and is then caught around the waist and lowered back to the ice.

## Star lift

In this spectacular lift, the man puts his hand on his partner's hip and lifts her above his head. The man holds one of his partner's hands as he lifts her in the air. He can then let go so that he holds the woman up with just one hand. She positions her arms and legs in a split scissor position to make a star shape.

throw jump

lasso lift

twist lift

star lift

# STEWART FEINSTEIN

Leading international figure skating coach, Stewart Feinstein trains skaters in London, England, and Colorado Springs, Colorado. He turned professional at 21 and has toured with the famous *Holiday on Ice* show. Read on to get the lowdown on how to be a skating star.

## How did you get into skating?

I started at 13, and everything about skating fascinated me. I loved what you can do on the ice, and I couldn't get enough of it! In my teens, I began having one-to-one lessons, and in my early twenties, I turned professional by touring Europe in *Operetta on Ice*.

## What makes a top skater?

Firstly, you have to have dedication. Skating is not a sport you can learn quickly. Secondly, you need to believe in yourself. Jumps require mental ability. If you don't succeed at first, you have to pick yourself up and try again until you do.

## How can I fall without hurting myself?

Falls are all part of skating, but if you feel that you're going to fall, try to relax into it. If you stiffen up, you are more likely to hurt yourself. Just imagine you're falling onto a soft carpet. Remember to tuck your fingers in. You don't want another skater going over them!

**Stewart *(right)* with international skater Jono Partridge**

## What's your favorite skating style?

I'd have to say freestyle. Successful freestyle skaters have to keep pushing the boundaries of their abilities. Top skaters perform jumps such as a triple axel and a quadruple jump in a program. You can't afford to stand still.

## What's the first thing you teach total beginners?

It sounds funny, but I teach them to stand on the ice with heels touching in a V shape, keeping their body weight over their feet, and their knees bent. They then start lifting their feet up and down and moving forward. They can then learn to push off on the inside of the blade to give power to their forward movement.

## Why do skaters wear such glamorous outfits?

Dancing on the ice in particular is all about drama and storytelling. A skater's costume plays an important role in helping to tell a story. It combines with the spins, jumps, and steps to make a complete performance.

# THE BACKFLIP

The backflip is a move that brings the audience to its feet. Former gymnast and French freestyle skater Surya Bonaly *(right)* is famous for landing the backflip on just one foot. She is one of the few skaters in the world able to do this.

## Essential technique

- Speed before takeoff
- Momentum during somersault
- Precise landing

28

## How it's done

1. The skater starts by moving backward. She begins at one end of the rink to build up speed.
2. Keeping one foot on the ice, she swings the other leg back behind her and then brings it forward again quickly.

The momentum starts to tip her body backward.

3. As she begins to somersault, the skater rotates as quickly as she can. She lands on the same leg she was skating on before the backflip.

## Why do it?

The backflip is one of the most exciting and acrobatic moves a skater can do. However, you are not allowed to perform it in competitions such as the World Championships and the Winter Olympics because it is so dangerous. Skaters such as Surya Bonaly use it in exhibition shows and professional events.

# SKATE SUCCESS!

Check out the youngest, fastest, and most spectacular in our roundup.

## Top scorer!

**Who:** Yu-Na Kim
**When:** 2010
**Where:** Winter Olympics, Vancouver, Canada
**What:** Most points scored in the Winter Olympics
**How:** Entered the *Guinness Book of Records* for the highest points total ever achieved by a female skater at the Olympics, with an amazing 228.56 score!

## Schoolgirl superstar!

**Who:** Tara Lipinski
**When:** 1998
**Where:** Winter Olympics, Nagano, Japan
**What:** Youngest individual Olympic medalist
**How:** Won the ladies' singles figure skating gold medal at just 15!

## Spins per min!

**Who:** Natalia Kanounnikova
**When:** 2007
**Where:** Rockefeller Center, New York, New York
**What:** Fastest spin
**How:** Broke the world record for the fastest spin ever recorded—308 revolutions per minute. That's over five spins per second!

## Champ jumper!

**Who:** Kurt Browning
**When:** 1988
**Where:** World Figure Skating Championships, Budapest, Hungary
**What:** First quadruple jump landed in a competition
**How:** Landed the first ever competitive quad—in which a skater spins four times before landing!

## Golden feet!

**Who:** Gillis Grafström
**When:** 1928
**Where:** Saint Moritz, Switzerland
**What:** Three consecutive gold medals
**How:** Won three gold medals for Sweden in men's figure skating at consecutive Olympics—from 1920 to 1928. Norwegian ladies' singles skater Sonja Henie performed a similar feat from 1928 to 1936.

## Super spins!

**Who:** Lucinda Ruh
**When:** 2003
**Where:** Chelsea Piers Sky Rink, New York, New York
**What:** Most continuous spins on one foot
**How:** Set a new world record by rotating an impressive 115 times on live TV!

# GET MORE INFO

## Books & DVDs

Freese, Joan. *Play-by-Play Figure Skating*. Minneapolis: Lerner Publications Company, 2004. Find out what it takes to become a skilled skater in this step-by-step guide.

Hill, Anne E. *Michelle Kwan*. Minneapolis: Twenty-First Century Books, 2004. Read about this popular and graceful skating star.

Hill, Anne E. *Sasha Cohen*. Minneapolis: Twenty-First Century Books, 2007. Learn more about this fiercely competitive U.S. skater.

*Learn to Ice Dance*. DVD. Queensbury, NY: Sharper Edge Productions, 2009. Professional ice dancers teach the basic patterns, timing, and techniques for beginning ice dancers in this DVD.

*Skating through Time*. DVD. Stamford, CT: Ten Mayflower Productions, 2005. This DVD profiles various famous U.S. skaters during the U.S. Figure Skating Championships.

## Websites

**Ultimate Skating**
**http://www.ultimateskate.com**
This website offers instructional DVDs licensed by the U.S. Olympic Team and uses technology and education to advance the sport of figure skating.

**U.S. Figure Skating Association**
**http://www.usfsa.org/**
This website is the official home of U.S. figure skating, both at the competitive and recreational levels. Go here to find clubs, coaches, events, and stats.

# INDEX